PRICKLY MOSES

By Simon West

PRICKLY MOSES

Poems

Simon West

Princeton University Press
Princeton & Oxford

'Three Poems after Franco Fortini' is based on translations from *Tutte le poesie* by Franco Fortini. Permission for use is granted courtesy of Mondadori Libri. © 2014 Arnoldo Mondadori Editore S.p.A., Milano. © 2015 Mondadori Libri S.p.A., Milano.

Published by Princeton University Press

41 William Street, Princeton, New Jersey 08540

99 Banbury Road, Oxford OX2 6JX

press.princeton.edu

LIBRARY OF CONGRESS CATALOGING-IN-PUBLICATION DATA
Names: West, Simon, 1974– author.

Title: Prickly Moses: poems / Simon West.

Description: Princeton: Princeton University Press, [2023] | Series: Princeton series of contemporary poets | Includes bibliographical references.

Identifiers: LCCN 2022056480 (print) | LCCN 2022056481 (ebook) | ISBN 9780691250595 (paperback) | ISBN 9780691250922 (hardback) | ISBN 9780691250960 (ebook)

Subjects: BISAC: POETRY / Australian & Oceanian | POETRY / Subjects & Themes / Nature | LCGFT: Poetry.

Classification: LCC PR9619.4.W46 P75 2023 (print) | LCC PR9619.4.W46 (ebook) | DDC 821/.92—dc23/eng/20230207

LC record available at https://lccn.loc.gov/2022056480

LC ebook record available at https://lccn.loc.gov/2022056481

British Library Cataloging-in-Publication Data is available

Editorial: Anne Savarese and James Collier

Production Editorial: Theresa Liu

Text and Cover Design: Pamela L. Schnitter

Production: Lauren Reese

Publicity: Jodi Price and Carmen Jimenez

Copyeditor: Jodi Beder

Cover image: John Wolseley, *Natural history of a sphagnum bog, Lake Ina, Tasmania*. 2013 watercolour, courtesy of the National Gallery of Victoria, Melbourne.

This book has been composed in Adobe Garamond Pro and Scala Sans OT

10 9 8 7 6 5 4 3 2 1

FOR MAGICA AND ANITA

CONTENTS

PRICKLY MOSES

NOTES ON CLOUDS

Imagine clods released to weightlessness,
        loft-drifting in a dream, greeting light
like tulle. Or else—still fanciful—sea's breath
        rising like a delivered soul. Then delight
for their hold on all four elements. Take rain,
        how moisture globes around a speck of dust.
Or fire, kindled in air's skein,
        it cracks against an anvil made of mist.

I used to watch that mirrored ocean foam
        float in slow motion over plains vast and rambling
as a pelagic vista, the crickets' metronome
        set largo fortissimo, the Goulburn untangling
north to the Murray—the valley's one clear border.
        The clouds moved east and drew your eye in their flanged
wake like a lure in whose shine you saw Dookie, Benalla,
        and a sweep of land to the Dividing Range.

Later I loved the high-rise fleece in old
        Venetian oils: your gaze drawn up tiers
of rough-hewn fog that angels scale
        like go-betweens. They bridge the stratosphere,
freeing the bounded eye to rise like Dante
        when he glimpsed the whorls of the empyrean,
or Armstrong breaching the Karman line to plant
        a leaping empire's footprint on the moon.

Seen from gravity's slant: hulls in ether,
        courts of quintessence sailing earth's personal
space. You look up to ask what's in the weather—
        watching them bank and breach,

or spread like locks on a barber's floor,
      or lour like a lid of slate. They can glow
with the longing of soft-fleshed fruit
      or the petals of a loose-stemmed rose.

The colours of clouds speak loud at dusk,
      and the omens you hear tell of uncanny squalls
as Gaia reorders her patterns of water and dust.
      Tonight they burn like windows in a banquet hall.
Hermes leans out, his head heavy with drink,
      and marvels at his bygone urge for human form.
That I have seen him is due to clouds:
      these mid-air inklings, clusters, constancies.

BODY'S KEN

As songs without words
run loose in the mind
and thoughtless as light over matter

so unruled lines will slip their moorings
and carry the eye on a current
that laps the shape
and crease of things.

Sometimes language lags
in the wake of body's ken.

Look how a sketch set down by hand
will draw you out like a walk
and into the park of flesh.

So still-life bottles talk to a bowl
and get the gaps between known things
as air takes shape in shadow and light.

So singing is good
when the sense of sound
comes divined in the throat

or the ear's chamber lets you float
half-buoyed in a fathom of waves.

To follow the threads of sight and sound
you're swept like a plumb
from the boat's hard rim.

So laughter will burst and sighs seep.
And breath is always there
as a breeze flouts frontiers.

A PENNY FOR YOUR THOUGHTS

It's a sluice whose gate is hard to shut, a stream
that has no source or mouth and buoys the rushing
ego in its wake, or else it's the ease
and glibness of the id. I love those leaps
of logic, like rapids over rocks, when the sound
and shape of words let slip new schemes of thought.

It's that monologue where all the head's a stage,
the chorus that foresees the worst, the run-through
where your wit enchants the empty stalls.
It's the homily that's preached each day by Doubt,
the waterboard debriefing with Regret,
that whispered invocation in a prayer.

It's a thread let drop and snatched up heedlessly,
it's the only outlet shyness will permit,
also known as the coward's stumbling block
or hurting no one but yourself. A broken
bridge, or a brackish well you cannot trust.
It's wind that stirs reflections in a pool.

THE CAMPANILE

Old stairs pitched steeply round an open heart,
rigged to walls by worm-holed traves,
girders and joists as thin as stilts, and landings
like the platform an acrobat might use. Trusting
to each hung step as though we trod on unlit
yards of air, we climbed alone, with hunched
and blinkered gaze set on the rung
below our feet. My bearings spun
like an arrow round a wheel. Rare slits
flashed on a foreign world. It was like a well,
this stair, built not to arrive somewhere, but to mark
how climbing we ascend out of ourselves.

And then above our head the door.
We rise where four arched openings gape with wind
and glutted light. No words but steadfast awe
at what sustains our weight and floods the swimming
eye—the tower's long-held poise, a hand
held up to test the air.
There, heedful as a statue that commands a room,
two bells hang like weightless rock
absorbing light's tide in downcast crocks,
storing it like a vessel from where
song breaks and expands
evening and morning and at noon.

WRITING SOUNDS

First the sound graphite makes drawn across paper:
a rustle like a dog circling in to nestle, or a tight-lipped
whisper as trance-like a child traces her name. The pencil labours
onwards but keeps manically crossing itself, as it plots its pitching

tracks in snow, or shuffles insect antennae into drift lines.
Then the bristles-sweeping sound, the rub-of-rosin sound, as the side
of the hand jumps like a wren in dead foliage, frightened
by the apparition of each new word. And finally

the swish of fingers tugging or run through hair.
Sounds like a eucalypt's new growth stirring and other such holds on wind,
or a clock's mechanics, but scuttling and erratic, like air
exhaled of a sudden. Sounds of the quelled set free,

of something quavering into shape. Psalms
to mark small victories.

IMPROMPTU PARADE

Scored for syrinxes
shrill as the screechy end
of an E string

a fanfare of semiquavers
by the local escadrille of eastern rosellas

coming in low in
full-dress dreamcoats
on a feast-day fly-by.

ACANTHUS

Without truss or strut beyond the base the stem
has surged upwards like a guyless pole.
The stele braces growth as bone depends
on sinew's give to lift a walking soul.

The flowers round that spike spread like a chorus
of suckling mouths. The petals grope
at light or gape like angels in their orders.
They shoulder out from elongated caps

as dark as mussel shell. Inside, each stamen
writhes like a wave or a whip caught on the rise.
And there, hovering in shadow, without strain
the anthers wait. They need no eyes

or memory. They hold no thought
of gain, but are the host that must be sought.

IN THE PO VALLEY

Rising after a troubled night
I stood by a window at dawn.
Two persimmons that gripped a leafless branch
above old ground a farmer had turned
so fallow earth might breathe, were set against
a snowy range that shone like an altar in lace.

No more. No less. But as if arranged
by . . . what, the light and its brief grace?
The blood pulsed and the mind came clear
like a nest in a winter tree. I wonder,
was I right to let such things declare
last night was just a dream?

THREE POEMS AFTER FRANCO FORTINI

Flames

I wish you could see
how the sky has cleared here, and the way
the roof tiles just abide, and the care
of the creek whose water is warming.

This is the word: spring exists,
perfection joined with imperfection.
The hauled boat's hull
soaks in the wood oil, the spider spins.

We'll save for later all that must be said.
For now, look at the shape that oleander makes,
and the flames of the magnolia.

27 April 1935

I would have been staring at a rose bed from the
window of my high school.
It was thirty-five years ago. That day
eighty thousand workers were inaugurating
the metro they had built in Moscow
in splendidly-lit rooms.

An author who's dead now once sung their praise.
I've read those poems. I've translated them.
I used to ask those white roses for love.
The white and the yellow roses. The city was clear.
Yearnings in the air. Horace sharp and bitter.

O eighty thousand workers of Moscow,
History has a foul way of laughing.
You didn't know. I didn't know. And the roses?
They don't want to know anything. The idle roses.

Response

He was lying on the trunk we kept in the corridor,
curled up like some wounded animal.
My mother was trying to help. Dino, please
get a grip, your son's watching.

While his eyes sought me out to ask forgiveness,
mine I've always kept open.
And I hadn't heard those voices again.

Now they call me
—not gently, not cruelly—the grey voices.
In answer to their whispering,
in the calm that follows weeping,
I offer this my response.

THE SUN IN THE DOOR

As gum trees seen through morning fog
dispute for us the fate of Job

so Roman ruins stay the sky
and animate our inner eye

the plum branch leaves the trunk behind
to stretch within a frame of mind

the hawk that's lost behind a hill
speaks to vision's mounting will

inklings jolt the ordered brain
like water struck by heavy rain

and riddles and linked rhymes set free
reason's hounds to chase a key

so nursery rhymes and playground games
allude to death by other names

and wits that come unmoored in sleep
ride heady currents out to sea

as light and shadow cross the floor
so archways frame an open door.

HEADING NORTH THROUGH THE GOULBURN VALLEY

I

It's summer's end and you're led back home
down tracks as plumb as higher laws.
From the carriage you scan colour-sapped
stubble—the wreckage of fields
that plot ground cracked as a bare heel.

Omen-wary, eager, you skim inexorable
lines. Lookout and helmsman, you sniff
familiar weather. After the far
meander routes you full-circle like the stock
of fate, you lap at memory rock.

Crossing the wracked and shadeless stretch,
the sweep of sun and sky-dropped
heat gulfs—your eyes tight reins—
you seek relief in horizon clumps
—the brakes of box and river gum.

The bush is a hobbled pre-settler aegis,
river's buttress, hanging on, hoping
to fill it all with fish, this cove of parched air,
to turn it to loaves, this hard-loamed valley,
till all's wed to the customs of shade.

II

The arrogation of greenness, elders
smile, inured to miracle.
The wide-eyed here soon learn to squint.
But still at journey's end that bosk
is sky prop and soul squat.

Later you'll sit on those banks, the heart
calming like a cup skolled in homage,
as if manumission might lie
in letting clutched weight fall away.
You'll rise, then, appeased and stiff as fashioned clay.

Crossing the last bridge into town an offhand gesture
loosens longing. From the train you watch a pitched core
plummet like a sinker. The thwacked
water will settle. Apple trees grow
wild along the tracks. Windfalls see us home.

VARIATIONS ON THE WALK BACK FROM BUSHRANGERS BAY

I

From headland rock
we'd watched up close how water can charm its own weight,
and the racing suck of foam over basalt.
We'd plundered the mirrors of stiller pools,
and roamed the clash and heat of the shore.
Now they were calling us in.
Above the wind they urged us for home,
spurring our march up the scarp,
up to the forest rim,
and in through the keeling facade
where stands of banksia and manna gum
guarded the spoils of shade.
It was cool inside
and held its scents like a room.

If you stride on ahead, that's a vanguard of one.
You can run under shoals of foliage.
On gums, leaves hang like the shreds
of canvas sails above a shipwreck
of fallen sticks and ribboned bark
that are pitched about the bole;
or where there is loose new growth
they catch the light like a crowd
of scimitars in the breeze.

II

The land that bound the bush
was bare and undulant and rose
from the ocean with furrows
and waves still on it.
Sheared and fenced, it has
the folds of corpulent flesh.
Erosion has carved out gullies
so each rise
curves on itself like a limb.

Looking out as the path skirts
the forest's edge
you can see how cleared earth
unrolls its acres of chroma
like a patchwork.
Then you turn inward again
to the intimate world of manifold
things. Here, in the bush, each floodlit
break in the piggeldy
tints of taupe and sepia
is stark as a spotlight. Better
to dash across gaps like cracks in the world.

III

Halfway along was an old eucalypt,
a black gum, with branches too stout for the trunk.
They grew parallel to the ground, twisting
like wrist joints in an artist's folio.

This tree has a hive in the mouth of a lost limb.
Bees fly from that seat like envoys embarking
to far reaches where she-oaks rouse
when their branchlets get tipped silver and yellow;

or through the fern and muttonwood that formed
the thicker undergrowth. There spilt light
falls and skitters like beads of water
over a sheen of dark green oil.

This gum had the gravitas of a well-climbed oak
and kept its watch and ward on a secret store.
Passing, you felt subject to its sovereignty,
and the onus of making wonder known.

IV

To reach the car
in fifty steps
will mean I'm meant
by fate to be a poet.

That was the lot
you dealt yourself, at what,
thirteen? Top of the last slope
you gauged the distance down.

Then leapt. Each stride
propelled by the hill, each foot
fell with a jolt
too wild to call iambic.

It kept the count, though,
like an earthen knell,
as you toyed with setting
whim in stone,

keeping delight
alive beyond
the bitumen
that breaks good spells.

EXEAT

Memorial Hall

First there's finding a place, but the pews are full.
Faces swill in the channels between rows and red
ties flash where boys vie for room.

When the masters march in under military flags
a thousand pupils rise in league. So must you.
You think of a herd in line to give milk.

Now the hymn begins and you see a boy
pitch his voice as if he were hurling a stone.
The organ tugs it back. Some chords

echo as the next one drones. *And did those feet
in ancient times walk upon England's mountains
green?* Don't utter *lamb of god,* and be wary

of word-spells hiding in hymn. The portraits
of principals tilt out from the walls.
Like a lake their faces are caught

in a gaze you can't meet. The shield
has a crooked cross, and a burning
bush above which *Deo* and *Patriae* and *Litteris* hover

like bits of ash in a flue. But these are words
and must mean something too. Now your eye
rests in the chancel's fluted windows. Vertical

pools of colour. Here the mantles of saints
shine like Pre-Raphaelite knights, but their features are faint
where ropes of sun pull taut across the hall.

House

At the end of the afternoon to climb the hill
to the boarding house there are stairs. They pass
under an alley of elms that are stencilled

against a leafless sky. In the dining hall the noise
swarms like a bee trapped in a jar. If you feel
sorry for it a pit opens in your stomach, and a voice

lists all that was given up back home.
Is it your father's voice? No. Just a voice.
When you sit at your cubicle in the study hall

it's like wearing a pair of blinkers. Your gaze tunnels
to the swim of words in your book. Unseen around you shouts
and the thwack of a ball against a wall. A thud as something
    heavy falls.

Chock Shop

A roommate's kindness can be meant in jest.
That first morning they tried, 'West!
Your uniform.' 'But it's Sunday.' 'Der! All newbies

wear it Sundays.' 'Really? Ok.' When you comply
they snigger, but when your trust wavers they're deadly
earnest. You guess this is some sort of test.

Friendliness is letting you share in the outburst
of glee as a kid on the stairs cops a hard shoulder.
'Get back to where you came from, Wang!'

Somehow it is worse for Asian kids. 'Let's
take West down to show him the chock shop.'
'But hang on, this place is fish and chips. You said chocolate.'

Lymphad

What creeds get sipped from the brick and glass of that hall?
Keep up the noble record of the past.
But distilled through unease and greed till all

prior things turn to an easy liquor of enlightened
hope. The lymphad on the coat of arms is urged
into the wind, its heavy canvas rolled. Rivalry

like a whip kept us rowing, that and the corrosive fear
of letting elders down. Ulysses' dogged
confidence rose on each hymn to the cell of the ear.

To strive, to seek, to find and not to yield.
To be experts of a world laid bare like a beach
by night's tide. The past was sealed,

a sheet where light will flicker in a swell.
Or else it was waiting like debris along those wild coasts
in Stevenson's tales, longing to be seized. We saw how the sand

received the imprint of our first feet,
and we ranged its length like scouting dogs
expelling scent on coiled seaweed,

high on adrenaline, running with the same
eagerness that Adam might have known
as he granted each discovered thing a name.

Broken River

Leaf litter. Layers of it. Lying in wait.
Gum leaves like crescent mouths, a motley
of forgotten names. The dryness of bush in late

summer. The scents of rising oil, my eye
running along filigree lines of shade,
scanning ground for cleared patches the size

of a foothold, working my way across bush,
our stretch of floodplain, to the river. Once, with Scotty,
home for holidays, we walked down to the Broken to fish.

At our backs that bush holds us in its gaze. A threshold
of complex striving things—the tentacles of liana,
the trees' wizened knit of leaves and sticks. A world.

He tells me stories of pig hunting up north.
I watch the muddy brown of water, the waltz
of shade over surface, the skitter of light like a birth

of pearls. And all the time with our rods
we divine a realm made opaque by the current's
load of loam, trying to play god.

Palace

Then words *set you going like a fat gold watch*,
words unearthed like a cricket that trips
across the flats of your wit, leaping just out of reach.

Like a chance gift they quickened the pulse, a gift the mouth
strove to unwrap. As the tongue went prodding the crease
of a consonant and felt each zephyred vowel,

a flood was released from its sluice, filling a plain
like winter rains, a field made a mirror, and for days
there were sproutings. Old seeds redeemed.

You swam in the streams of poetry. You entered its halls,
its courts and its cells, a barefoot boy eating
with kings. From high casements you gazed on the world, saw

rhyme locked in dance with reason, and the mantic rain
that kept you circling back to certain lines.
As in Agatha Christie, order and mystery shared the refrain.

You paid homage in stilted rhymes—
melancholy tight-packed into a final foot,
the autumn breeze blowing out its open-ended line.

Like household gods above the coals of a hearth,
Justice and Progress, the Rightness of our Time,
were the idols you kept chatting in your head.

Cellular

When you wake from that trance, where do you belong?
The school hall. Hemmed in a pew. Squirming
like something a fisherman bears in a net, undone

by the lines people you live alongside
haul in. Companions. Family. Caught
in that swell of sea and rope and tide.

He locks himself in a bathroom. Like a hermit
in the cradle of his cell. Anywhere. At large
or in the boarder's toilets just to escape the restless street,

and the passage of unacknowledged faces. The chipped host
of the mirror hangs before him. He stares till the swim of thoughts
settles and rippled water reveals a form lost.

But what sort of life is this? Huddled
in a cubicle, the white walls yellow
with the damp of a daily summary clean, and the grout

blackening the frame of each tile's dull sheen,
and mould eating the loose rolls of silicone
cowering in corners like earth-seeking vermin. All the signs

of the morning's former visitors challenging an outcast's
bower and precarious control. Each muddied
print left by a gridded sole, a menace

like a snag that makes a current eddy.
It points to someone who's made their choices,
who's left their mark and can hold their head high.

Home

Coming home for the longed-for long weekend, it was the train
delivered us to old worlds. I gulped the light at dusk.
Light that swirled round boles of shadow, or scrubless plains.

Up here you swam in land's loose psyche,
felt the rightness of place, felt colours and sounds
and smells flooding the senses' unlocked dykes,

land throbbing like a bee's dancing abdomen
as it tests the air for flight, or the bob
of the kingfisher's beak as it hunts from a snag.

I sat by the stream, teetering between will
and a lull that let you dwell in mystery,
that strange poise that brushes like a silk

shawl the hardening intellect, or like the ripple
of the rainbow trout that nudges the clouded
surface from below, letting your eye dance round the tip

of a form that widens as it disappears.
And it seems now the narrative was identity. It's always
the same hidden campaign led by fear

to forge distinctiveness. To trust
both rage and sober thought,
to heft the gifts

of home like a totem, holding good
to how the woods took shape when words
stirred in the crucible of love.

Like the season's raw memory, leaves layered on land,
lanceolate fingers, palms keeping time to the cicada's
bourdon, pressing at the underside of a blank canvas.

The river shucks in each indent of eroding bank.
Its surfeit of tongues lap and forget themselves,
easing into the slick of surface, then rising to lap

again. Up here you carry in your chest like a smouldering
sphere a sense of bygone endless things.
It was stoked by the hum of the mouthless bush where it shoulders

its joules and buzzes like high-voltage
cables catching static in the rain.
An onus that wants to be told.

Snap

It was the sharpness of a close-up portrait I sought.
A face caught by surprise. The smile the camera fixed
jumps from the mouth to the dilated eyes. I stalk

through a background's blurred layers of bush,
then my gaze returns to settle on my father,
not lost yet but caught here in the past,

in a moment of pathos at the end of exeat,
when the horn of the diesel train keens for departure.
That moment when you can almost touch loss, and the next

best thing to holding it is to point the camera.
Photos? You'd think this was bye forever, he'd said.
Later I stared at that snap, hoping some dicta

might emerge from those lips, the way an image floats
through liquid to surface on the page. I've tried
to go back, to take hold of such forms like a ghost.

VILLEGGIATURA

After Rilke

Again and again we walk out
though we know this view so well,
the outlined ridge that keeps its snow,
the churchyard with its names in stone,
and know the cleft in the mountain
and our fear at night when we fall.

Again and again we walk out together
leading our joy like a child
down the alley of chestnut trees
and the path that climbs above the town
till we reach a field of day-long flowers
and lie to outstare the sky.

ELEMENTAL SONG—YARRA BEND PARK

I wonder at the windways water carves,
has always carved in loam,
river's running vein, glossed glass

that gives back bush cross-sectioned from those mud-packed joints
down to her threadbare baldachin. Water taut in a flute,
the top brushed silk whose shine

is bent around each fold or, under wind,
will ripple through riddles forged
faster than starlings on the wing.

Current works a slower change. Surface plots
of shadow pulse for it,
and pulse for what

rides roughshod down below—the silt-thick puzzle
of an unseen realm.
The eye leaps and tacks and straddles

old lifeways of land, rich recess
kept for selving rites and what . . .
Sunday idylness?

Kingdom of increase, welcome this song and be slow
to grant our clearings. Like a twofold child I'll hold
to your spell, though I'm pulled up short now by Heidelberg Road.

PADDLESTEAMING

In Echuca we walked out on the three-tiered wharf
built of red gum sleepers and facing north,
its back butting the bank's dun cliffs
so the sun streamed through those columns and traves as if
we were moving through a Piranesi print,
some labyrinth of the past, some etched glimpse
of darkened stairs and landings shot through with beams
of light so thick and busy with motes it seemed
you could grasp them by sticking out a hand. We tried.
You can't. But loosened minds can turn a tide
and slip through time to a time when people rode
on steam-run paddles down a watery road.

Earlier we'd stopped at a spot on the Campaspe
and pulled from our borrowed car a rug and esky
and spent a while watching time head north from high
up on a cliff where the bank was eroded by
that silt-thick water that caught the light like a latte
in its glass back home, and just for a laugh, eh,
we lobbed down fist-sized stones to make a splash
but then thought, don't, when two mallards dashed
out skirting the water, wings spread, so for a sec
we gazed on the brilliant stripes of blue in their speculum.

Now it was our turn to step out on a mirror
not of feathers but an element still unfamiliar
and just as good at flight. The boat's engine
below was a furnace fed wood, and the paddles trenched
the water like a famished dog, but up on top

we floated and saw the world unfold its plot
at a pace more suited to a dream. Our heads turning
like clown heads at a show, amazed by each yearning
tree's one-off statued stance, each bole
with its quirky iter upwards—marred by a burl
where wood's grains had surged like a wave to close a wound,
or swerving as if caught ducking a punch or in a swoon:
stations on each living and many-armed cross.
Some trunks open homes to galahs where a limb lost
makes a door, or to the sulphur-crested cockatoos.
Both birds, as if they had nothing to lose,
are quick to burst on the wing into raucous screams,
their white forms more agile than the puffs of steam
the boat's chimney released, but I preferred
the shrill toot of its whistle to those of the birds.
It was joyful, like a herald with good news,
like the water itself that tacitly hollers, hey youse,
rallies all life to its source, says, slake on that.

This fluent cross-country doodle is also a magnet
and the sole magnate of neighbouring lands,
for a hop skip and jump past the Murray, it's just sand
and plains of saltbush scrub to my eye. The sky
runs an extra mile to meet the ribbon of the horizon
and snugness is the hood of a car. So we cling to the cortege
of reflected light, this baptist whose largesse
speaks for an ampler religion than the human heart,
harder too, and not one from which you can part,
though acolytes of speed and noise still try.
Like the nave of a church that has doffed its roof to the sky
when it empties, quiet follows the speedboat's water-quake,
and we're lulled by the sideways waves of its wake.
Sure, theirs is a rite, but so, without mercy, is war.
The hometowns of my youth passed on a rough kind of lore.

Dream-like too was how from the boat the banks
seemed so close and yet out of reach. We sailed aslant
from time and place. So by way of Aeneas in Dis
I recalled my father, who brought us here as kids. This
was his river and while Red Cliffs is a bit downstream,
the same red gums grip the eroding edge, the same gleam
of sun splits the surface. Light's tricky to harvest,
but the grapes his father farmed, though the yakka was hard,
perhaps they seemed like a yield of sun in good years.

Years makes me think of how we marvelled at the sheer
age of trees we'd seen that morning at Barmah.
The girth of some trunks dating them back further
than Dante's seven-hundred rings. This selva
was more open, but had an eeriness too, under a spell of
dry, awaiting the kiss of floods to revive,
while up in Canberra the alchemists connive
over elixirs that ensure water's rehashed
before it gets here, not as wine, but cash.

Red gums, still? You'd think I'd done that trope to death!
But why be coy about obsessions? The heft
of trees outgrows my thoughts, each trunk bears more
than I can understand. Up close to the moorings
of exposed roots, a new leaf, and limbs that interlink,
the mind widens like a canopy. While it shrinks
when things are only known exclusively.
The simile's our modus operandi.

And so water leads to poetry—that source
of words swelling to a flood, though flames, of course,
are also kin to speech (take tongues). We get
from the fluent elements our tropes for chat,
while earth keeps its stony silence, though the mount

of Parnassus was rock, and I reckon we're more grounded
walking on poetry's feet. Language's true grace
is to be still and in flight like the Victory of Samothrace.

But nearer to now and to home we came in to dock.
The swallow sitting on our flagpole's stocky
head till we'd lurched on the current an hour ago
reclaimed his spot. On shore your legs grow
with the land, not rooted, but buoyed on the arch of feet.
And so we were back where two waters meet:
the Campaspe, née Yalka, till Mitchell and the state
married her to a mistress of Alexander the Great,
and the Murray, Dungala, whose many lost lives
I wish sailing the past could redeem from earth's archives.

PRICKLY MOSES

On the growth of an Acacia verticillata *planted the year before.*

Our loose-limbed wattle, our lounger up heights
is gaining leanly to the rungs
of lesser trees

and has struck this spring
her first nuggets of gold, is letting branchlets
roam like tendrils and clamber light like a rope.

We slacken the eye in your pool of green
needle after needle, evergreen, monogreen,
crosshatching space till a painter would puzzle

to botanize a branch with a fuzz of petioles
or go for a Green Knight with red wall poking through.
Prickly Moses,

when I think how long I ignored your name
to marvel at ash and oak and elm,
I guess we're still shy of the Promised Land.

Like way back when our foreign forebears the squatter
and illiterate wit coined your common name,
cutting mimosa down to Moses,

and reckoning your type by laying hands on a limb
to pluck a sapling for a fishing rod,
and you were found wanting to homegrown wood.

You grow regardless. You obtain, lopsided,
the enlightenment of well-pitched things, your equilibrium a wry smile
beaming in an old bloke's bristly face,

as I pass you on the pathway at the bottom
of the stair. Your first commandment:
start out from acknowledgement.

A CATALOGUE OF WATERCOLOURS

Three skulls. And then a melon cut so we see
    a slit of reddish pulp. Here's a scatter of half-sketched
pears—they hover on the inkling of a plane
    and hoard their stock of colour like a keep.
Now the ansa of a jug—chipped and nondescript—
    set close against the night-sea of a wall.
And, look, woven in a cloth, leaves and curling stalks
    that warp across the valleys of a crease.

But the shutter of the sky's too wide. I'm struck
    by how these objects of the earth run thin
in water's element. Some hardly reach
    the surface so the paper seems a sunlit creek.
I imagine piners turning in the higher orbits
    of paradise. Their forms set free, their faces
crystals shot with radiance. And I long
    for something with its feet set on the ground.

In this one, where we get a glimpse down the alley
    of an unkempt park, it's not a break
of redgums along the fenceline of a paddock,
    and the sky and stone are hardly home. But I think of you.
You're swimming in the fringe where light turns back,
    shade like a stoup of undiluted colour
that spills from foliage on a stand of chestnut trees.
    And I recall how poems cast good shadows too.

IN HILL COUNTRY

*And people go marvelling at high mountains, and huge waves, and
wide-flowing rivers, and the spread of the ocean, and the course of the
stars, and look not into themselves.*
                                    Augustine, *Confessions*

Watching from the pleat of a tectonic plate
        a far range pucker the horizon
                I'm reminded
how so much happens at the back of vistas
        in hill country.

You can trace a road
        over loose folds of land
                only so far as a tuck or a lee.
Suddenly your eye is leaping
        to pick up the ribbon a mile off
where it skirts the midriff of a neighbouring rise.
        What have you missed?

A track through upland bush,
        having crossed a crest with its spike of scrub and rock,
the next minute
        has you down in the damp of fern and moss
where creeks run covert
and the blackwood and ash form a frieze
        that shifts as you walk.

        In hill country
lands overlap like a conjurer's hands. Stare all you like,
        as he settles those three cups
his bunyip has fled the thicket's near rim,
        and entered the run of a further gully.

How many vanishing points!
How many windbreaks for the mind to vault!

Piedmont tractors rake furrows
      like a comb through unruly curls,
leaving the seams of land
to collect old species
      like fluff in a pocket's stitching.

Late summer.
      Among far hills' stubble
      patches of green settle in dips
          like water pearled in the sling of a leaf.
For every slant of evening light
that drop comes back refracted.

Plains give too much away. They take glib to a new level.
And though weight, like rain,
      will roll off the back of a well-worn brae,
where the forehead of earth is furrowed
      I'm put in mind
      of thoughtfulness.

When Petrarch reached
      his mountain top,
lands fell in the sweep of his eye.
      The sea shone back like a mirror. So much
      got ratified.
He wasn't in hill country.

Here
      each rise
leads to another. Few
      bother to rank heights, or boast of ascents.

As you walk among hills
      you forget the boundary
      between one crease and the next.
Your feet rise
then fall, jump
      and fall, till you've left behind
the simpler allegories
of altitude.

BACK ROADS

Back roads out of townships leave on loose ground,
stray from old stockyards or the end of the shops,
or outgrow streets skirting the cemetery and tip,

and just keep running along crackling bitumen.
Back roads down country that farms grip
roughly in patchwork fists.

And always, driving, that strip where your eye bobs,
that shaw of thick-boled redgums and new growth forming
a stand against the fenceline of paddocks.

Fullness sidling along earth kept bare, brim lines
ample with shade and the play of light through leaves.
Box trees, their bark rough as dry grass,

and a flock of grass parrots grazing for seed
and the mat of twigs and dropped leaves underneath
scattered like paint dregs on a studio floor.

Affluence to set against vistas of stripped turf,
and the brittle clods kicked up by passing cattle.
Till miles off you meet

the next old name on the map,
or the turn-off tried once
as a short-cut to the highway heading south.

ROADSIDE SHAWS

are the leavings of larger woods, still sturdy
as if bush had been freshly cross-sectioned
and all we have left are these strips.
You think of the tips of roots talking
as they ramble under cleared ground or tarmac's
no-growth zone to twice the width of a crown,
meeting down there the stock of forebears
cut when the forest got hit by the stump-jump plough.

And you puzzle at the scraps and strips of bark,
the sticks and confetti of dropped leaves
spread like a charm at the feet of steady creatures.

Shaws like a shrine that ushers the mind round boundaries
and down paths of once and what if,
into the lands of wilder plenty.

THE COLLAR PIECE

From a park bench,
tired of the glories of Rome,
I watched the sequinned sheen
in a pigeon's collar piece.
Like the sea at rare times it shifted
between hues of mauve and green.
As the pigeon neared my feet
I saw how he kept
wings clutched to his side
just as a stranger, passing
through a market, might hold a bag.
His coo was harsh like a corporal
commanding a parade, when what
I had wanted
was the elation of a *cooee* as it echoes off rock,
a voice playful as that collar
snicking bits of light.
I lashed out with the tip
of my shoe. And now it was
water wended to wine:
those wings clapped air
like barefoot kids racing
to the top of a travertine stair.

GHIRIGORI IN TURIN

I'm fond of learning. Now these country places and these trees
won't teach me anything, while the people of the city do.
                                        Plato, *Phaedrus*

Because the flagstones are smooth like calmed water
          and contain the colours of dawn.
Because the buildings are tall as mature woods
          and their facades lean in like whisperers.
Because the point-lobed domes of the plane trees
          are a spinney above the Dora's stream.
And the courtyards are clear as an amphitheatre,
          and out of the mouths of rooms
          voices run like a clattering herd.

Corralled in stone's old lap
          speech has the softness of flesh.

Because green arabesques
          will swirl in the margin of vellum.
Borage and mallow and old man's beard
          prodding, unshakably as spring,
          the ploughlines and postils of the almost everlasting.

NORTHERLY

As water sweeps fast from under the fins
and bellies of fluvial things when a river
or torrent swells with spring rain,

so now the slow-stirred pool of air
that cupped earth's nook like a cupola
is scattered by the wind. Home's

fixed spot on the map is blown, and the suburb's
measured step to the hills comes undone.

All morning some far-off god of the north
has harnessed loose ropes of air
to run horizontal.

I imagine a snake whose underside catches
the tops of trees as it slithers in flight down the plains,
but really it's all head-first careering
and mouthless as a magnetized ball
that is eager to nudge the Antarctic pole.

Even with four walls wrapped around me like
a hooded coat, my thoughts are sucked outside
where they're gripped by the plot of our eucalypt.

Great tufts of that tree are caught in the drag of sky's
tide and undertow.
I catch my breath as I listen
and wish I could skip straight to the verdict of evening.

WILLOWS FELLED ALONG MERRI CREEK

Back then willows were old-world self-seeders.
Left to themselves, they had flourished like weeds
and I loved the slant and turn of their trunks,
the weird arcs suckers and offshoots made
out over space like an open vault,
and how each spring leaves turned a limb to a cave.
Where we entered, up on the underside
of that low-hung roof, a scaffold of unsteady shine
bounced off water in the creek, so shade
in its deepest pockets was skittish with light.
Swallow-fast shimmer in bits, sibyl-like speech,
the impressed passion of a dream. To prize and set against
the harder forms of things that still remain—
like fences, now of picket, now wire lace.

LOOKING SOUTH FROM TASMANIA

This is the encircling river that outgrew myth,
that drops in one leap to the Antarctic pole.
Water too sheer for Neptune, more like a rift
in our maps. Gormless, gelid, whole.
Seen from space it swaddles the earth,
but here, watching surf whip a rim of basalt cliffs
you weigh up submerged wrecks
and the bob of ice over light-starved depths.

Out there to be tugged by that muscle of wave
would strip the mind of its glint and leave you huddled,
heart-first, in the scapula's cave.
Out there, southerlies nock up arrows of air
to loose at the shore. Spit flicks your cheek
and you're deaf for the rush of wind at your ear.

EARSHOT

I'm in earshot just as the garden's hit by a breeze
and the eucalypt sounds like sand or grit
that's trickled through a fist to sprinkle the ground.
Leaves hang loose on the gum
and for each quick brush of wind
knock like abutting boats
or get tossed in the sway
of a shimmering pendulum.
When the wind is strong
I remember whole clumps of that green
turn dark and thrash in time
like wrack in a wave that captures the attention
and draws you to harsher thoughts.
But now's the time for lighter sounds,
whispers, echoes, rain on glass,
background things half heard and overlooked,
whose loss alone makes clear.

LATE-WINTER BLACKBIRD

Merle, I marvel at all that you are
and the marl of your song that is never spun
how it trickles like water fronded with foam

I love how your voice looks up like a child
climbing to a crag-top shrine

as you sing no less
than iliads of here and now

and I approve your preference for grace notes
and how you pause at the end of each line
which shows a theologue-like thoughtfulness

how you'll sing at ease from an eave or an ash
but prefer this year the perch of our gum

and your low profile outside of matins and compline
and your faith that all this will work

how just on the edge of earshot
from an oak at the end of the park
your echo is singing a song of his own

how all this from the black pith of your coat
from the pit of your gut
from the thrall in your throat
is urged on you
and will not be explained.

SETTLED RAIN

Spring rain
shed from cloud that spreads its ash-milk
stains of watercolour across the suburb's hills and plains.
Clouds passing low like a parade to the wind's baton, to the
crackle of brittle water on panes.

Cracks of tiny tinny walnut shells
or metallic pearls. Each drop recast by what it hits.
Here, stuck to the coaxing gravity of glass,
they worm downwards
and light pools in their portly half.

Settled rain. Not heavy, not light.
And not drizzle or spit, but tipped
by a steady hand from the wide head of a watering can.

You tickle attention. You draw us out
of stagnant barracks and dens of thought
into the fluid home of air.

The green of nearby evergreens
is darker now, and the new shoots
on the ash trees in a row down the road
are someone caught stark in their underwear,

and light doesn't filter through the paws
of eucalypts now. They've grown tight-fisted and
ragged as a cormorant.

And the spire in Clifton Hill is our frontier now—
its bluestone has thinned to a silhouette's monochrome
and is grainy as mist.

And the tar of the roads has spread its silver net
and fishes for photons
that swim in great schools, and eagerly
slip from your clutch on the sheen of their bellies.

And the hills out east and the city have gone
and we're snug in our keep that has climbed
into the womb of the sky.

NOTES AND ACKNOWLEDGEMENTS

Prickly Moses is the common name given to a number of acacia species in Australia, in this case the *Acacia verticillata*, a small tree native to southeastern Australia, in places where many of these poems also have their roots. These lands were long held by the Boonwurrung People and the Wurundjeri People in areas occupied by the city of Melbourne, and further north around Shepparton and up around the Murray River by the Taungurung and the Yorta Yorta People. I pay my respects to these traditional owners, and their elders past, present and emerging. Other poems run like the Po River down from the Western Alps and through the northern plains of Italy. 'Three Poems after Franco Fortini' is based on Italian poems from Fortini's volume *Paesaggio con serpente* (1984). 'Villeggiatura' is based on Rilke's untitled poem *Immer wieder, ob wir der Liebe Landschaft auch kennen*. In Italian the noun *villeggiatura* describes a holiday away from the city, in this case in the mountains near Turin. In 'Exeat' italicised phrases include quotes from Blake, Tennyson and Plath. The poem 'Paddlesteaming' recounts a trip on the PS Alexander Arbuthnot on the Murray River at Echuca. Dungala is the Yorta Yorta name for the same river in those parts, as Yalka is for the Campaspe. The epigraph to 'In Hill Country' comes from Augustine, and runs in the original, *et eunt homines mirari alta montium et ingentes fluctus maris et latissimos lapsus fluminum et oceani ambitum et gyros siderum, et relinquunt se ipsos* [*Confessions*, Book 10, 8, 15]. In 'Ghirigori in Turin', *ghirigori* is the Italian word for doodles or arabesques, but can also mean meanderings, labyrinths and eccentricities. The epigraph by Plato runs, φιλομαθὴς γάρ εἰμι· τὰ μὲν οὖν χωρία καὶ τὰ δένδρα οὐδέν μ' ἐθέλει διδάσκειν, οἱ δ' ἐν τῷ ἄστει ἄνθρωποι [*Phaedrus* 230d].

PRINCETON SERIES OF CONTEMPORARY POETS

Printed in the USA
CPSIA information can be obtained
at www.ICGtesting.com
JSHW020911250823
47226JS00004B/5

9 780691 250595